BRITAIN IN OLD PHOTOGRAPHS

BISHOP AUCKLAND

CHARLIE EMETT

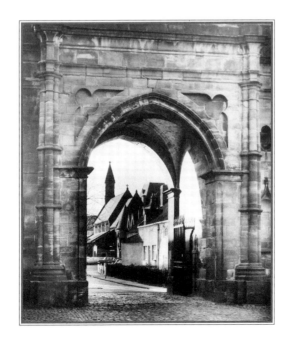

SUTTON PUBLISHING LIMITED

Sutton Publishing Limited
Phoenix Mill · Thrupp · Stroud
Gloucestershire · GL5 2BU

First published 1999

Title page photograph: Looking towards
Bishop Auckland market-place with
St Anne's church prominent, seen through
the massive Neo-Gothic gateway to
Auckland Castle.

British Library Cataloguing in Publication Data
A catalogue record for this book is available from the
British Library.

ISBN 0-7509-2072-6

Typeset in 10.5/13.5 Photina.
Typesetting and origination by
Sutton Publishing Limited.
Printed in Great Britain by
Ebenezer Baylis, Worcester.

A C K N O W L E D G E M E N T S

For permission to rummage through the *Northern Echo* picture library, I am indebted to
Andrew Smith, Editorial Director, North East Press. For their great kindness, unstinting help
and excellent coffee, I thank Peter Chapman and lovely ladies Jane Whitfield and Christine
Watson, competent guardians of this treasure house. My thanks to the Revd John Marshall,
Vicar of St Andrew's with St Anne's church, Bishop Auckland, and his delightful lady wife; and
to Mrs Nancy Ashton for enlightening me on Bishop Auckland's sacred and secular
beginnings. My sincere thanks, also, to Christina Blythe, Deputy Head of King James I
Comprehensive School and to Gillian Wales, Manager of Bishop Auckland Town Hall and
Grand Vizier of The Hog Wild Tent of the Sons of the Desert. To Ellen Rutter, my thanks for the
typing. A very warm thank you to all my friends at Sutton Publishing, especially Simon
Fletcher, Alison Flowers, Joyce Percival and PR expert Rebecca Nicholls. It is a terrific boost
being part of such a great and very professional team. If I have omitted anyone, it is
inadvertent and I apologise. As always, any errors are mine: I've got to be responsible for
something!

To some people like Cecil
Lawton, its chairman,
pictured here on
26 February 1986, the
RAFA Club is a logical
extension of their RAF
days. The mural of
Liberators on a raid is a
tongue-loosener; and
many exciting tales of
derring-do are spun
within the club's hallowed
walls. I salute all RAFA
members and those who
'gave their tomorrow so
that we could have our
today'. I, too, proudly
wore a uniform of blue;
but it was a deeper shade.

CONTENTS

On 29 February 1984 Cockton Hill School celebrated the seventy-fifth anniversary of its opening. Here the infant school's pupils, in period costume, re-enact school life during its first year, 1909. It was built in 1908 for 1,200 pupils and was the largest school in Bishop Auckland. At that time Bishop Auckland had several educational establishments, the largest, until Cockton Hill School was built, being St Anne's National School for infants and girls only. It was built in 1855. In 1858 a Wesleyan school was built in Russell Street to accommodate 350 children. By 1910 it had become a Council school and the Methodist school was housed in South Church Lane in huts behind the Grammar School. In 1861 a mixed Roman Catholic school was built in Hexham Street. It housed 400 children.

INTRODUCTION

Set on a steep bank above the River Wear halfway between Darlington and Durham, Bishop Auckland, the seat of the Bishop of Durham, is a busy industrial centre with a history as long as its origins are shadowy. The 'Auckland' part of its name may be a corruption of 'Oakland', or 'Parkland', but is more likely derived from the Viking 'Acler', meaning land added to an estate. 'Bishop' denotes its ecclesiastical connection.

During excavations at the Roman camp and administrative centre for the region, Binchester (*Vinovium*), a mile east of Bishop Auckland's market-place, Stone Age artefacts and evidence of Bronze Age and Iron Age settlements were found.

Binchester covered 9 acres and was built by Julius Agricola in AD 80. A significant domestic settlement was attached to the Roman camp, which probably continued unchanged for some time after the military abandoned the camp in AD 411. Bishop Auckland's strong link with the Romans is still evident today. Its main thoroughfare, which ends where Newgate Street enters the market-place, follows the route of Dere Street, the main Roman road from York to Corbridge.

The Saxons captured most of Britain during the fifth and sixth centuries, and although there is no evidence of a Saxon settlement in Bishop Auckland itself, nearby Escomb church dates back to about AD 675 and is Saxon. It was built during the early years of that period of history considered to be a time of intellectual darkness, the Dark Ages.

It is not possible to date exactly when Christianity was first planted in Britain, but the presence of British bishops at the Council of Arles in AD 314 is evidence that an organised church existed at that time.

At the end of the tenth century the See of Lindisfarne was removed to Durham and a cathedral was begun as a shrine for the relics of St Cuthbert. Bishop Carilef began to build the present cathedral in place of an older one in 1093, and replace the secular clergy with a Benedictine community – which lasted until the dissolution of the monasteries in 1540.

In about 1016 the Danish King Canute gave the lands around Auckland to the See of Durham during the episcopacy of the first Bishop of Durham, Aldhune, who is credited with building the first ecclesiastical house in what is now Bishop Auckland.

When the Domesday Book of 1086 was compiled, the ancient Kingdom of Bernicia or North Northumbria was not included. This comprised all the land north of the River Tees. Bishop Hugh de Pulset's assessment of Bernicia's land value appeared in the Bolden Book of 1183, and Bishop Auckland was, by then, important enough to be mentioned in it. Now it was the administrative centre of Aucklandshire, which consisted of North and West Auckland, Escomb and Newton.

At different times during the twelfth century large areas of Bernicia were cordoned off as deer parks for the Prince Bishops of Durham. In about 1183 Bishop Pudsey built Bishop Auckland Castle, also known as the Bishop's Palace, a manor house and hunting lodge which has been altered and added to on many occasions since. In 1350 the deer park, or Bishop's Park as it came to be known, was enclosed by a stone wall; Auckland Castle has been the seat of the Prince Bishops for 800 years.

Today's market town of Bishop Auckland originated as North Aclet settlement, which developed into a typical Durham green village, sited on high ground 100 ft above the south bank of the River Wear. Houses circled the green, their individual outhouses and enclosures radiating outwards to a defensive wall. The village developed eastwards until it reached the enclosure wall of the Bishop's Park. Thus the original settlement of North Aclet became joined to the ecclesiastical complex of Auckland Castle and its ancillary buildings. Until the mid-nineteenth century Bishop Auckland had served a mainly agricultural and ecclesiastical community and the population of about 3,000 had remained fairly constant for generations. Then came the Industrial Revolution and everything changed. The demand for minerals led to the rapid expansion of the railway system throughout the region and within twenty-five years Bishop Auckland was the hub of a complex railway network that served Weardale and the surrounding areas. The region was opened up as never before.

During the 1860s there was an influx of new materials such as Welsh slate for roofing. New techniques in glassmaking meant that different styles of windows could be introduced and Bishop Auckland developed its own distinctive style, using curved glass in bay windows. Poor quality soft local 'seggar', black-centred brick, was replaced by glazed brick from Bedfordshire, and hard-fired, smooth red brick from Yorkshire and Lancashire was also introduced.

Sited at a meeting of many routes, Bishop Auckland made an excellent centre for commerce and trade. By the final quarter of the nineteenth century many of the manufacturing and service industries were dependent on local natural resources and this encouraged further mineral development in the surrounding district. Iron ore, limestone and fluorospar flux were all brought in from Weardale and the Cleveland Hills by train. Specialised clays were needed for the brick and vitreous china industries, and nearby Witton Park needed large amounts of coal for its iron and steel industry.

Bishop Auckland stands in the middle of a coalfield into which, until the 1870s, there had been few deep sinkings. Usually the shafts were no deeper than 350 ft. They were worked by a gin and a horse and output was small. Then, between 1872 and 1876, there was an unprecedented development of the coalfield, the collieries were enlarged and output shot up, exceeding 1,000 tons per day in some instances.

During the latter half of the nineteenth century Bishop Auckland expanded rapidly southwards, spreading along Dere Street, its main approach road. Close to the town centre housing development took the form of closely packed, brick terraced dwellings with larger, mainly stone-built terraces sited further out. Grander, mainly detached houses of varying styles from both the Victorian and Edwardian periods graced the town's outskirts. These were built to last by master craftsmen and still look impressive today. More recent development has been in the form of estates grouped along the town's southern perimeter.

The town's focal point is its market-place to the right of which, when approached from Durham Road, is the neo-Gothic gatehouse leading to Auckland Castle. Two splendid buildings, the magnificently restored Town Hall and adjacent St Anne's church, dominate the market-place: sacred and secular side by side. The facilities of the Town Hall are named after people who have brought pride to Bishop Auckland: people like Stanley Jefferson who, as Stan Laurel with Hardy, made the world laugh, and Sir Edward Elgar, who composed wonderful music.

Bishop Auckland Football Club, founded by ordinands from Auckland Castle in Bishop Lightfoot's time, is sited to the south of the town next to the cricket club. They are football crazy in Bishop Auckland and have named a street after their most famous player, Bob Hardisty.

Bishop Auckland continues to change with the times, moving confidently into the future from an honourable past. When it was a village, people called it 'Auckland'; now it is a thriving market town people call it 'Bishop'. Perhaps this augurs well for the future.

CHAPTER ONE

HOME OF THE PRINCE BISHOPS

For almost 300 years Auckland Castle or the Bishop's Palace has been the principal country residence of the Bishops of Durham. Bishop Pudsey built it as a manor house and hunting lodge in about 1183 and it became the chief seat of the rich and powerful Prince Bishops of the Palatinate. Although sited on a defensible loop of land between the rivers Wear and Gaunless, the castle was not primarily a stronghold. Bishop Pudsey built a grand Banqueting Hall there in the twelfth century, complete with a buttery, wine cellar and minstrel gallery.

For almost 500 years the Prince Bishops of Durham dined and entertained guests in the building. Bishop Beck built a two-storey chapel near the castle's entrance screen, but it was demolished during the Civil War. Following the Restoration of Charles II, Bishop Cosin took possession of the now delapidated Auckland Castle. Cosin, devoted to English church traditions, converted the Great Banqueting Hall into a chapel and joined it to the rest of the castle by a connecting wing which provided the entrance to both. The roof was heightened to form a clerestory, which greatly lightened the building's interior, and made it the largest private chapel in Europe. St Peter's Chapel was consecrated on St Peter's Day 1665.

In this picture St Peter's Chapel, viewed from Wyatt's Wall, has about it a romantic quality that is irresistible.

Leaving the Bishop's Park, 6 August 1961. The castellated gateway is crowned with a turreted clock and a weather vane, which was designed by Sir Thomas Robinson of Rokeby in about 1760 for Bishop Trevor, whose incumbency there was from 1752 to 1777. The much older clock was originally housed in one of the clock towers which surmounted the main wing of the castle and dates from 1474. The former Park Gate Houses on the left were formerly occupied by the staff of Auckland Castle, and date from the early eighteenth century.

Looking out from Auckland Castle gateway, with its vaulted ceiling, 5 March 1969. It was never designed for defensive purposes and has never had to act as such.

Looking in through Auckland Castle gateway, 8 June 1970. It is summertime and the tree in the foreground is in full leaf. The Elizabethan building through the gateway on the right is the Castle Lodge.

The Castle Lodge is an excellent example of Elizabethan architecture. The door encasement and the square stone mullioned windows of this fine three-storey seventeenth-century building blend harmoniously with its cobbled forecourt, and the overall effect is greatly pleasing.

Looking through Wyatt's Wall, a decorative screen built in 1796 for Bishop Shuke Barrington, towards St Peter's Chapel. His coat of arms and the diocesan coat of arms are on either side of the central arch. A chapel, built by Bishop Anthony Bek (1284–1310), stood on this site until the Civil War, which was a disaster for the bishopric. Under the Commonwealth the episcopate was abolished and the castle sold to prominent Parliamentarian Sir Arthur Hazelrigg, who was a Puritan and against the finer trappings of the Church. He demolished Bek's chapel and with the materials set about building himself a mansion in the grounds. It was never completed because Charles II regained the throne and Hazelrigg was committed to the Tower. That year, 1660, Bishop John Cosin, a great churchman and a born architect, came to Auckland Castle, demolished the new house started by Hazelrigg and started to spend an enormous sum to restore the castle to its former dignity.

The northern aspect of St Peter's Chapel seen as background to the Bishop's Park, 1964. The park was enclosed in 1350 by a stone wall, which originally contained fallow deer, fish ponds and rabbit warrens to provide game for the bishops. In 1627 a herd of thirty-two wild white cattle was housed there. During the Commonwealth the park contained no deer, no usable timber and little other wildlife. Following the Restoration the park began to restock with deer.

The River Gaunless, the loiterer, flows through the Bishop's Park, emptying into the River Wear just outside the park's enclosure wall. The undulating, mature parkland of the Gaunless valley is magnificent and many unusual tree species are found there, including Corsican Pine and Sequoia, which Jeremiah Dixon brought back from North America. He it was who landscaped the park and straightened the Gaunless.

Born in nearby Cockfield, Dixon, a self-educated mathematician, found fame when he and Charles Mason surveyed the disputed boundary between Maryland and Pennsylvania in the USA in 1763–7. This became the line which divided the free states in the north from the slave states of the south – the Mason–Dixon line.

The deer house in the Bishop's Park, *c.* 1895. It is now in the care of English Heritage.

In the heart of the Bishop's Park, the deer house makes an attractive picture in the snow in February 1985. The house was erected by Bishop Trevor in about 1760. It was designed as a cloister with arcades facing outwards to shelter the deer. The central courtyard was used as a feeding place, while the tower was an ideal place for hunting parties to rest.

Following the Restoration, Bishop John Cosin set about converting the Great Banqueting Hall into a chapel, building up interior walls above the arches to form the clerestory to enhance the appearance of the outside and the lightness inside. The raised roof was now 64 ft high. He added the richly ornamental ceiling with his heraldic arms, criss-cross panels, cherubs, mitres and an eagle in the centre. The columns supporting the arches consist of two shafts of local Frosterley marble and two of sandstone. He joined his new chapel, St Peter's, to the rest of the Bishop's Palace by building a connecting wing which provided the entrance to both. He raised the floor with its present black and white squares, added the Sanctuary steps in marble and the communion table, all seen here.

CHAPTER TWO
HEAVEN'S DOORS

The hill on which St Andrew's church stands may have been the centre of a Christian community since the eighth century. The present church was built in about 1274 and is a cruciform, 157 ft long, with the width across the transepts being about half its length. The original lighting was by lancet windows and the architecture was early English. In about 1295 Anthony Bek, Bishop of Durham, carried out extensive alterations, added the south transept and raised the outer walls of the aisles. In 1417 Cardinal Langley, then Bishop of Durham, had the handsome choir stalls made, raised the chancel walls, added the clerestory in the nave, and added a battlemented stage to the tower and embattled parapets to the chancel and transepts. In 1894 the present chancel arch replaced the original lower and narrower one. In 1881 the organ chamber was added and the south transept rebuilt. In 1926 the south bay of this transept was re-consecrated as a war memorial chapel, particularly for the 6th Battalion, Durham Light Infantry. The old aumbry has been fitted with a glass door for the Book of Remembrance. St Andrew's is probably the largest parish church in the diocese.

Inside St Andrew's church, looking towards the altar, 1989. The fine nave has five bays, the richly moulded arches being supported by alternate octagonal and clustered piers. The stone head of King Edward I projects from an arch on the north side, top left.

The finely coloured stained glass windows of St Andrew's church date from the church's nineteenth-century reconstruction. The vicar's car once had a stained glass window: a blackbird did it.

Effigies of a knight, *c.* 1340, and of a lady, are thought to be connected with the local Pollard family. The knight is carved from oak and his feet rest on a lion which has been roughly carved into a boar. In legend one of the Pollards received a grant of land after killing a wild boar. However, the fact that the lion has been reshaped suggests that it was altered to fit in with the legend: Hutchinson, writing in the 1780s, says that the knight's feet are resting on a lion while Richley, writing in 1872, describes it as a boar, so it seems that the effigy was altered between these two dates. The knight's real identity remains unknown. The lady probably dates from about 1500 and is thought to be one Margery Bellasy.

The Saxon cross incorporates fragments of one that was nearly 1,400 years old, and the presence of a Saxon cross in the church indicates that the hill on which St Andrew's stands may have been the centre of a Christian community since the eighth century, though it is likely that the cross was a substitute for a church rather than part of one. The depiction of St Andrew on the cross links Auckland with Hexham, a principal site of Christianity in eighth-century Northumberland. The crucifixion scene depicted on the cross is that of St Andrew, not of Christ. The fragments of the great cross of St Andrew were assembled in their present form in 1938. It is one of the finest examples of eighth-century Saxon art in Europe. The font is modern, donated by W.H. Knight in 1939.

The outer doorway of the south porch in autumnal sunshine, 17 October 1991. In the Middle Ages it was customary to hold weddings in church porches, and this may explain the relative grandeur of this part of the church. The base of the holy water stoup can be seen in the north-east corner of the porch, and over the porch entrance there is a sundial dating from about 1749. (See page 13.)

The Revd John Marshall, much-loved vicar of St Andrew's church, pictured on 29 November 1994, standing at the inner door of the main entrance, the south porch, one of only two in the diocese with a room, once the vestry, above it. (See page 13.) The porch is Early English in style, divided into two bays and noted for its fine vaulting. The porch is more ornate in style than the rest of the church, and contains three Early English style windows. The arches are not the original ones: they have been renewed in sandstone. There were originally two pairs of heads, each pair representing a knight and his lady, on both the outer and inner doorways. Those on the inner doorway remain and one is seen left of and slightly above the vicar. Those on the outer door have weathered away.

In September 1987 St Andrew's church was the setting for a highly successful programme of *son-et-lumière*, when the story of the church and the town of Bishop Auckland was told by means of light and sound. As the fascinating history unfolded, the audience was able to see the church literally in another light.

Son-et-lumière at St Andrew's church, September 1987. Here, like hymns ancient and modern, an ancient 'ka' park accommodates a modern car.

The St Andrew, Auckland, Company of the Church Lads' Brigade, 1937.

Rising like a beacon above its surroundings, the tower of St Andrew's church is a reminder that the church plays an important role in the life of the area as it has since St Andrew's was first founded. The traditions established over so many centuries are still being maintained and today, more than ever, the church looks outward to the community and involves itself in society in a way which would have amazed the priests who celebrated mass in St Andrew's during the Middle Ages.

St Anne's, top right, has never been a parish
church, and no district has ever been
assigned to it. In 1782 the Governors of
Queen Anne's Bounty created a perpetual
curacy there and since 1804 every vicar of
St Andrew's parish church has also held the
perpetual curacy. Not until 1867 did the
churchwardens of St Andrew's become also
the churchwardens of St Anne's. Previously
St Anne's was served by chapel wardens.

It is not known when St Anne's church
was founded. The present fine nineteenth-
century church is the successor to at least
three chapels on the same site, the first of
which was well established in the late
fourteenth century. It probably originated
some 200 years earlier when the great
Bishop Hugh de Puiset (1153–95) made his
manor house at Auckland.

Members of St Anne's Church Friendly Society, known as the GFS, *c.* 1934. The occasion was a
pageant to celebrate Empire Day and most of Bishop Auckland's schools and youth organisations
took part. Miss New South Wales seated at the far right of the front row is Mary Stubbs who later
married, becoming Mrs Firbank of Hilton Road, Bishop Auckland.

St Helen's church is built of stone and dates from the late twelfth and thirteenth centuries. Its main entrance, the south porch, is reached through a walled churchyard from the busy Bishop Auckland to West Auckland road. The church has neither tower nor spire, only a bellcote containing two bells, one with a Latin inscription. The present bellcote replaces an earlier one that collapsed during a storm in 1832. One of the bells was cracked in the fall and had to be recast. When the bellcote was rebuilt the original bells were replaced.

The elaborately carved bishop's throne in the chapel in St Helen's, 1954.

The interior of St Helen's church from an old etching, c. 1900. The window at the west of the nave is made up of a group of three stepped lancets. Outside, a modern boiler house, made of stone with battlements and a pointed door and window, matches the church's original design.

The beautiful altar in St Helen's church. The clerestory of the nave is late Perpendicular with battlements (see page 21), but the aisle has none. Lady Sybil Francis Eden, who lived at nearby Windlestone Hall, is buried in St Helen's churchyard. She was the daughter of Sir William Grey and married Sir William Eden in 1886. Her son, Sir Anthony Eden (1897–1977), 1st Earl of Avon, was born at Windlestone Hall and became Prime Minister despite his father's hatred of politics.

Escomb church, built in the seventh century, is the best preserved example of a Saxon church in the country. It is one of the finest examples of early Christian architecture in Northern Europe. Many of the stones used in its construction came from the Roman fort of nearby Binchester (*Vinovium*). One stone bears the inscription 'LEG VI', indicating the 6th Legion, the 'Victorious', which was garrisoned at York in the second century. Escomb is derived from *Ediscum*, meaning a sheltered nook or dwelling place. The church's circular graveyard, or 'God's Toft', shows its Celtic origin. The church has an Anglo-Saxon sundial and a carved, stone altar cross. This photograph dates from June 1963.

The beautiful simplicity of Escomb church's interior, 1964.

The altar in Escomb's Saxon church, 1934. The extra large stones edging the chancel arch are set end up and alternately north, south and west. This is known as megalithic quoining and is a feature of Saxon building.

'All Things Bright and Beautiful'. Hymn singing by candlelight in Escomb church, Christmas 1994. A glorious blend of ancient church and modern worshippers that lies at the very heart of our Christian belief.

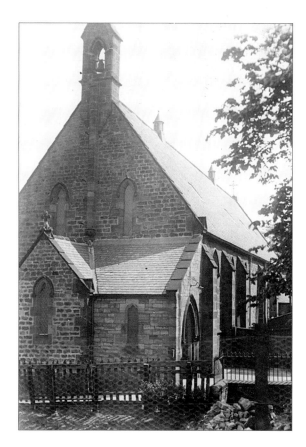

The first Roman Catholic service to be held in Bishop Auckland following the Reformation took place in the Assembly Rooms in Fore Bondgate in 1840. Now the Catholics have a church, St Wilfred's, in West Road. This is how it looked in 1939. It has since been enlarged to meet the needs of Roman Catholics from the surrounding catchment area.

The Society of Friends is at the opposite end of the Christian spectrum to the Catholics. A Friends' Meeting House was erected in Newgate Street in 1665, and was demolished and rebuilt in 1840. The fashionable wedding of a prominent Quaker lady, Miss Fryer of Smelt House, took place there in 1879, one of the guests being Mr J.W. Pease, MP. This photograph of the intricate adornment above the Meeting House doorway, surrounded by scaffolding, was taken on 18 November 1971.

Peter Edwards, Secretary of Bishop Auckland's Jehovah's Witnesses, seen in about 1970. In 1994 a quick-build structure was erected near St Andrew's Road on the Bishop Auckland by-pass. The foundations were laid and the building completed during one weekend by 350 workers, many of them craftsmen from the N.E. Community Project. A nearby school was hired for catering and, miraculously, the Jehovah's Witnesses' new permanent building came into being.

Bishop Auckland Baptist church is on Cockton Hill Road and has a tower. It also has a talented church music group, pictured here on 13 February 1996.

The Central Methodist church, pictured here in 1953, is now Bishop Auckland Methodist church. It stands alongside the Lady Eden Cottage Hospital, which was founded by Lady Sybil Francis Eden.

Bishop Auckland's Wesleyan church was opened in Newgate Street on Wednesday 18 February 1914, to replace an earlier one that had stood in North or Back Bondgate. The Methodist Society first worshipped in a room, part of a woolcomber's shop in Matthew Forester's Yard, behind Newgate Street. Their first chapel was built in North Bondgate in 1808 and was reputedly the largest meeting room in Bishop Auckland. From being a chapel, the North Bondgate building became an auction room, then a warehouse, before being demolished.

The opening of the Woodhouse Close Methodist church, Saturday, 24 March 1962. The Revd Michael Thompson is the minister in charge of this thriving church and community centre.

CHAPTER THREE

BISHOP'S HUB

North Aclet, the settlement from which Bishop Auckland developed, stood on high ground overlooking the River Wear, slightly west of the ecclesiastical complex of Auckland Castle. By the thirteenth century the village had developed eastwards and the basic layout of the town's market-place, between village and castle, was formed. With time, dwellings and a chapel developed along its periphery. The town's gaol was sited under this chapel and the stocks stood at its western end. In 1391 William Forster, John Chaloner and others took waste land at the eastern end of the chapel and Cardinal Langley granted a licence for the chapel to be rebuilt on it. The chapel was dedicated to St Anne. Permission was given to hold masses and other services on holy days but the congregation was limited on Sundays to the sick and infirm so as not to be detrimental to the mother church of St Andrew's. In 1452 the chapel was enlarged. This sketch depicts the market-place during the early years of the nineteenth century, with the chapel that preceded the present St Anne's.
The neo-Gothic gateway of Auckland Castle stands at the eastern end of the market-place and a shelter occupies part of today's Town Hall. The lady in the shelter will have to wait for more than a century before a bus turns up.

The years take their toll. Dwellings that, in about 1900, were habitable were in a neglected state by 1982, when this picture was taken in the market-place.

Among the sad-looking buildings in the market-place was this filling station with its antediluvian petrol pump, 1982.

The King's Arms, together with adjacent buildings of character, have transformed the north side of Bishop Auckland market-place into a most attractive area.

A fair in the market-place, c. 1905. These popular events were held regularly and attracted large crowds. In those days everyone wore a hat, even on hot summer days.

Market day, *c.* 1900, and everyone is wearing a hat. The hot potato ovens are in the right foreground.

The original design for Bishop Auckland Town Hall was by London architect John Philpot-Jones, for which he won £20 in the early 1860s, although it was never used. The one used and seen here in 1985 was a modification of the original by local architect John Johnstone. Neither architect was responsible for the road improvements.

Bishop Auckland Town Hall Council Chamber.

Bishop Auckland Urban District Council's chain of office, symbol of the local authority centred in the Town Hall, which was built to meet the need of an increase in population. Until then, social functions had to take place in either the Assembly Rooms, Barrington School or the workhouse; but by the middle of the nineteenth century this was becoming unsatisfactory. So in 1858 it was proposed that a Town Hall be built and a competition for a design was announced with a prize of £20 for the best one. A Londoner, John Philpot-Jones, was the winner, but his design was not used. During the building of the Town Hall it was struck by lightning, 'making the iron pillars glow'. There was no cash available for a Town Hall clock, so the ladies of the town collected for one, which was installed and lit by gaslight. But cash was available for a Turkish bath, which proved to be popular. The Town Hall was opened on 28 October 1861 by Colonel Stobbart. Bishop Auckland Urban District Council has been superceded by the Wear Valley District Council.

This is how the Town Hall looked 121 years later as the background in 1982 to an inspired bungee jump by fireman Tony Taylor, who raised over £500 for Michael Jackson, who had lost his wife and children in their house fire.

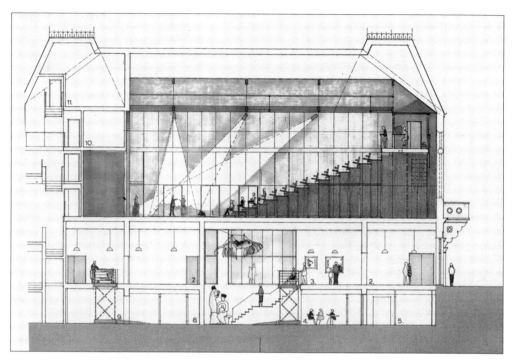

In 1989 the future of the Town Hall was in jeopardy when it came within an ace of being sold off to developers. A petition signed by over 10,000 concerned residents saved the day and a £3.2m restoration scheme was started. This is an artist's impression of how the renovated Town Hall would look.

During restoration work the Town Hall was under wraps, and is seen here in March 1992.

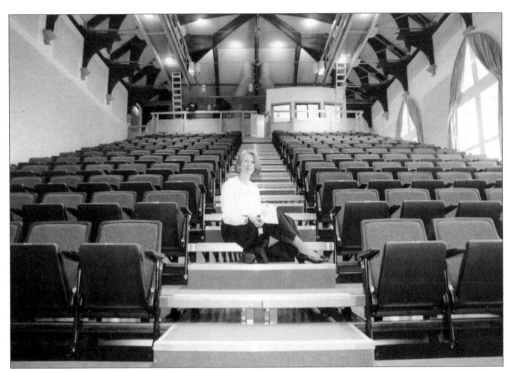

Here the beautiful and talented manager of the Town Hall, Gillian Wales, is pictured in the auditorium with its new seating. It is a very impressive sight.

The exterior of the building is also impressive. Following refurbishment, the Town Hall won an award, and it is now regarded as the jewel in Bishop Auckland's market-place.

Detail at the entrance to the Town Hall, which was
built in the Franco-Flemish style and originally opened
in October 1862. It was reopened in 1993 after a
major refurbishment.

Until the mid-1980s the street traders in Bishop
Auckland hired their stalls from Wear Valley District
Council. This view of the market-place, with St Anne's
church top left, was taken in April 1984.

Just as the Fat Controller regulated Thomas the Tank Engine, so the Market Controller regulated Bishop Auckland's market, the only difference being that the Market Controller, far from being fat and pompous, was in fact, in 1980 when this photograph was taken, a lovely, kind and helpful lady called Mrs Margaret Glen.

The market-place was refurbished in 1985 and on 17 May of that year the Town Crier, John Stevens, borrowed from Alnwick for the occasion, gave forth the news in ringing tones. From now on street traders would buy their own stalls and hire just the sites from the Wear Valley District Council. However, the *status quo* remained for some time.

In 1991 the market faced a takeover threat from a private company and the incensed stallholders gave vent to their feelings, protesting strongly. Here, Dave Burdon (left) and Les Wilson (right) appeal to shoppers for their support. Eventually the private company backed off and the site for the stalls remains with Wear Valley District Council.

Cause for celebrations and dancing in the streets. With commendable precognition, buskers Clive Nelson and Simon Porter begin the warmup – in January 1988.

Framed by skeletal market stalls, a couple steal a goodnight kiss. He whispers sweet nothings in her ear: she whispers sweet nothin' doing in his. Then the police send them packing to their homes.

There are places in Bishop Auckland more conducive to amorous liaisons than the market-place. Close by is the arboreal Durham Chare, a fine romantic spot. But sometimes love is blind.

CHAPTER FOUR

WHERE THE SHOPS ARE

Newgate Street, pictured here in 1914, is Bishop Auckland's main shopping centre and its building styles are as varied as its shops. The Yorkshire Bank, for example, is built in Jacobean-style sandstone ashlar and features a round turret with a spire, a very rare architectural style in this area.

McIntyre's shoe shop, *c.* 1900. It stood opposite the Yorkshire Bank and was a late eighteenth-century building with nineteenth-century alterations. It had a fine, oval shop front with curved glazing on either side and Ipswich-type glazing in the middle. Etam now occupies the site.

Gregory's, the Butchers, was established in Newgate Street in 1850, north of the Waterloo Hotel. It is pictured here in 1937. Behind the shop was a slaughter house which was entered through the Alma Hotel archway on South Church Lane. The Sanitary Inspector's report of 1909 was not very complimentary about the town's slaughter houses: 'There are eleven registered slaughter houses in the district. With three exceptions, they are placed most undesirably close to dwelling houses. Cement floors are required in two premises. "Blood holes" in two premises should be replaced by properly trapped gullies, placed outside the slaughter houses, and in nearly all premises covered, galvanised pails are required for the removal of offal.'

The Manners family had a butcher's shop in Bondgate during the latter years of the nineteenth century. In 1900 they moved to their present premises in Newgate Street. Today butchers do not slaughter their own beasts and hygiene standards are far superior to those of yesteryear. Here Betty Brown smiles broadly while holding a tray full of mouthwatering fare, 8 August 1996, having been with T. Manners for forty years.

Competing against 500 trainees on 60 Fine Fare schemes throughout the United Kingdom in a recruiting poster design competition held in March 1984, trainees at the Bishop Auckland superstore designed the best recruiting poster in the country. Six teenagers spent two weeks putting together the poster; personnel officer Shirley Bottomley said of them, 'We are delighted. Their efforts have certainly paid off. The youngsters put in a lot of hard work into the project and deserve a pat on the back.' Nothing like buttering them up!

Bishop's Bistro, pictured here during the 1920s, welcomes diners by the charabanc load. Central Methodist church, now renamed Bishop Auckland Methodist church, is clearly seen on the right. It is one of only a few Methodist churches in the region with a spire.

A floor higher than the ubiquitous 'Woolies', the nearby Co-op building dominates the centre of Newgate Street. Bishop Auckland Co-Operative Society was founded in 1860 and its full name is the Bishop Auckland Co-Operative Flour and Provision Society. It opened its first shop in South Church Lane on 28 May 1860, to counter the hold that the mine owners' 'tommy shops' had over the miners. The Society's first shop in Newgate Street opened on 2 May 1868 with a monster party: 16 st of flour were baked into bread for the 800 people who attended. The Co-Op, seen here on 2 November 1960, was built in four parts between 1873 and 1894 and is now a unified, fine stone building.

Duff and Rowntree's drapery, clothing and furnishing store dominated the junction of Newgate Street, Fore-Bondgate and the market-place during the early years of the twentieth century. It differed from Doggart's, another department store in the market-place, grandly called Auckland House in being more upmarket. A.L. Doggart developed his business from one founded on agents who went knocking on doors every week, collecting for the Doggart Club. Duff and Rowntree operated differently, catering for a more select clientele: they did not operate a club. As Doggart's business thrived Duff and Rowntree's failed. A furniture store, W.E. Gill, pictured here on 25 February 1964, became established on the Duff and Rowntree site. The building has now been demolished and Newgate Centre occupies the site.

An artist's impression of Newgate Centre from the north – the pedestrianised end of Newgate Street. The centre was opened in about 1980.

Newgate Centre, the inside of which is seen here, offers a new concept in shopping. Catering for the diverse needs of discerning shoppers and with an accountant's eye on profit margins, supermarkets like this one have mushroomed, providing an abundance of choice at competitive prices all under one roof. As a consequence many small businesses and specialised shops, unable to compete on price, have been forced to close. All mod cons include a moving walkway for shoppers.

Closures are ongoing. Here, in July 1995, Ron Nichols stands outside Seabreeze, a wet fish shop in Newgate Street, which was up for sale. A hairdressing salon, Sacks, now occupies the site.

In 1985 Bishop Auckland's Fine Fare came third throughout the United Kingdom in the company's 'Butcher of the Year' contest. Here, David Neal, the store's manager, is being congratulated by Tony Craddock, Fine Fare's meat project director, on his fine achievement.

Newgate Street is not without its resourceful shopkeepers when it comes to fighting crime. The announcement displayed on the window of Pedersen's radio and television shop in October 1981 will come as a shock to would-be burglars!

It is 7 December 1967, and Newgate Street is lit for Christmas. This is make or break time for many shopkeepers, who depend on brisk Christmas trading to compensate for times when turnover is not very active.

Newgate Street, July 1962. From the 1870s until the present day thousands of miners' families from surrounding pit villages have done their shopping in Newgate Street and adjoining thoroughfares. Along Newgate Street in about 1900 there were 130 business premises including banks, hotels and pubs. Grocers and drapers predominated, but there were many other outlets, boot and shoe shops, milliners, bakers, confectioners, fishmongers, butchers and chemists. There were also many shops in the market-place, Fore-Bondgate, North Bondgate, High Bondgate, Low and High Tenter Streets, Princes Street and the east side of South Road. Wilfred Hartburn MP had a shop in Newgate Street; and one of the patent medicines he sold in 1900 was Hartburn's Phospherised Tonic, 'the greatest brain food'. Herdman's shop in Newgate Street had, at one time, been the Lyceum Electrical Cinema. It is now a video shop: *plus ça change, plus c'est le même chose*. The Depression of the 1930s hit Bishop Auckland seriously. Many shops closed. The only one doing any real trade was Carnforth's, who provided a valuable service during those hard times. Carnforth's was the local pawnbroker.

CHAPTER FIVE

WHERE THE HEART IS

Pleasant Leazes Lane at St Helens, Bishop Auckland, its verges aged with hoar frost, along which a young lady is walking in spring sunshine, symbolises the road to a rosy future for countless young, single adults who aspire to marry, purchase or rent a house, raise a family and turn the house into a love-filled home. For some, purchase is an achievable goal; for others, an unattainable dream.

For house purchases the first step is usually the building society, and Darlington Building Society has been well represented in Bishop Auckland for seventy years. Darlington Building Society is primarily concerned with providing home-buying facilities for South Durham and North Yorkshire, where more and more young and not so young couples are determined to have a house of their own and a worthwhile investment. 'Why pay rent when you can buy your own at the same of less payment each week?', they ask.

A delightful up-market residence on the outskirts of Bishop Auckland is Woodhouses, photographed in December 1968.

These bay-windowed terraced houses in Victoria Avenue are more in keeping with the pockets of most people. They are well-built and comfortable dwellings, much sought after – but having been erected before the advent of motoring for the masses, they do not have garages.

There is a refreshing lack of conformity about these dwellings in High Bondgate Street, west of the market-place, pictured here on 27 July 1994. They are all listed.

Leeholme, Mickle Grove, is a highly commended cluster of thirty-six dwellings with a warden's flat, commissioned by Wear Valley District Council, designed by the Napper Errington Collerton Partnership and built by R. and W.A. Johnson Ltd.

Four of the former Park Gate houses on the northern side of the approach to Auckland Castle gatehouse, seen to the right of the picture, have now been demolished despite a nine-year fight to save them. Unlike some seventeenth-century cottages to the west end of Bondgate, which had thatched roofs, these were roofed with red pantiles. In about 1956 Mr Desmond Roper, Managing Director of D.V. Roper Ltd, had plans to turn these historical buildings into a tourist attraction, but Wear Valley Urban District Council had other ideas. Eventually, in 1965, when this picture was taken, they issued him with a compulsory purchase order to make way for a by-pass; but the market-place, which fronts these now vanished dwellings, is pedestrianised.

Mean streets like South Terrace are a grim Victorian legacy found throughout the land. The bracketed street lamp is a reminder of those days of long ago when lamplighters were essential. The Morris Minor is indicative of the future: the street has been demolished and is now a car park.

Playing football in a quiet, relatively traffic-free back street is far from ideal. When this picture was taken on 27 July 1962 many parents were complaining about a shortage of playing fields in Bishop Auckland. Thirty-seven years later they still are!

Houses with gardens are not always traffic free. This one in Redworth Grove was photographed in July 1976: it was the fifth vehicle to end up here in eighteen months.

When council estates like North End Gardens were built, the quality of the materials and the workmanship left much to be desired. In 1977, when this picture was taken, all these council houses were scheduled for modernisation. This created a problem, because as soon as the occupants moved out vandals moved in.

Sometimes it is the council by its intransigence, not the vandals, that causes problems for its tenants. When in 1981 disabled widow Elena Peat, aged eighty-five, asked the council to complete repairs to her damp-ridden council house, her request was turned down.

Braving inclement weather in January 1988, Paul Cockerill, Chas Barthorp and Paul Love (left to right) wer campaigning to save eighteenth-century cottages for posterity. They were not successful.

The year is 1968, and night-shift workers in the Dent Street area of Tindale Crescent are unable to sleep during the day because of nois from the gas works, which has been there for years, noise free. Th problem is only four months old but, following an ancient law, increases in direct relationship to the complaints of the sleepless residents. Locally, sales of matche doubled until the problem was solved.

Henknowle Farm Estate was designed by McAlister Armstrong and Partners, commissioned by Wear Valley District Council and built by Shepherd Construction Ltd in 1978. There were 308 houses on the estate.

Contemporary housing of a contrasting style: Woodhouse Close. The arch on the right is an ornamental gateway to a private dwelling.

These tied cottages housed employees of Ferens Mill, and both cottages and mill have been consigned to history. The picture was taken in November 1969.

The outside remaining wall of the old Ferens Mill, 7 February 1970. In the foreground is the horse trough donated by the Bishop Auckland Temperance Society in 1873.

CHAPTER SIX

ENDEAVOUR &
SOCIAL SERVICES

Endeavour was middle-aged when social services was a baby gurgling in its cot. But time passes, and yesterday's workhouse is today's social security. Until the unprecedented development of the coalfield, which has Bishop Auckland as its centre, between 1872 and 1876 the local economy was rural. Farmhands lived in dwellings like Dell Cottage, pictured here on 10 August 1881.

Today Bishop Auckland is the local market town for a scattered Weardale farming community. Livestock trading took place here, at the town's cattle mart, pictured on 29 November 1960. Once the trade of wool spinning was carried out in the town. Slab-wheel spinning, a method of hand spinning, was common. On warm, sunny days spinners would sit outside their doorsteps plying their trade. The auction mart is still in existence at 5 Church Road.

In 1830 Ferens Bros established a flour mill in Bishop Auckland's Durham Chare; it later became a limited company.

The site of the Ferens flour mill was well chosen because Durham Chare is joined by Castle Chare, once the only road into Bishop Auckland from Durham and much used by horse traffic. The horse trough, seen here on 16 October 1963, stands at the bottom of Durham Chare and was built by the Temperance Society of Bishop Auckland in 1873.

In December 1969 fire razed the flour mill to the ground. So ended the last of a series of medieval flour mills along the River Gaunless.

St Helen's Colliery, seen here in 1841, is typical of colleries on the north-east coalfield at that time. Coal mining was the greatest source of employment in and around Bishop Auckland from the nineteenth century, expanding to a peak before the First World War when it produced 20 per cent of the national coal output. One local colliery Black Boy, changed hands several times during the mid-nineteenth century before being purchased by a north-country entrepreneur, Colonel Wood of Howlish Hall, who filled in the old shaft at Auckland Park and sank new deeper ones to reach the Brock seam at a depth of 160 fathoms. He enlarged the colliery, adding extra sidings, coke ovens and workshops. Colonel Wood also owned the collieries of Auckland Park, Westerton and Leasingthorne, all of which he sold to the Great Northern Coal Company in 1873. The new owners made more labour and money saving improvements and attempted to free the neighbourhood from unhealthy, noxious gases. Miners were moved from unlit hovels to houses with clean running water. Woodhouse Colliery workings ran underneath Bishop Auckland and caused damage to houses above them. Bishop Auckland was always affected by recession in the coal industry, many miners emigrating to America, Australia and South Africa where their mining skills were put to good use. During a major recession in 1926, 120 miners left Bishop Auckland for Chesterfield where they found work with the Stavely Coal and Iron Co. Following the Second World War the coalmines were nationalised; and now there is no mining around Bishop Auckland.

Some Bishop Auckland streets still had gas lighting in 1964 when this picture was taken. The lamplighter's face is a study of quiet pride in his work.

The roadman's job may be unspectacular, but it is thanks to his largely unsung work that the pavements remain safe for people to use. This autumn scene of Etherley Lane on 10 October 1972 highlights the problem, the solving of which people take for granted.

It is thanks to the endeavours of dedicated people like Bob Corkin of Shildon that much of what is Bishop Auckland is preserved, otherwise it would be lost for ever. Bob is an amateur photographer who takes pictures of buildings before they are demolished. Here he is, on 15 October 1981, at South Church Road, having taken a photo of Rossi's ice-cream parlour.

With this sort of work, timing is of the essence. Had Bob Carlin turned up for a photo session on 19 December 1983 he would have been cutting it fine.

Bishop Auckland's labour exchange was housed in this building, now occupied by City Electrical Factors. In its day it served the community well, as industries and the world of work changed out of all recognition. One of many defunct industries was tentering, a process of stretching wet woollen material over a series of small hooks, allowing it to dry without shrinkage. Victorian Tenters Street is named after that vanished industry. During the 1870s Lingford and Gardiner and Co. made Gardiner's patent spring-frame bicycles at their works in Railway Street. They were 'admitted to be the most comfortable yet brought to the public notice'. They and Messrs R. Wilson and Sons Forge and Steel-works were the two biggest indust-

ries in the town. Then there was Lingford's Baking Powder factory – which fronted a 'secret' wartime factory. It was situated in the United Methodist church at the south end of Newgate Street and produced camouflage netting. The workers entered it via Lingford's to confuse enemy spies. The 'secret' was the colour of the netting, which indicated where the next campaign was likely to be. Following the end of the Second World War the netting factory became redundant, and Lingford's Baking Powder Factory closed in December 1973. Down the years, with closures of large employers like these, the local labour exchange was kept busy.

The labour exchange is called the job centre these days. Here, on 18 April 1985, the Manager, Keith Greenwell, stands outside the Bishop Auckland branch.

Today's postal service has diversified tremendously, but not always without hiccups, like the one the Bishop Auckland branch had as recently as 1995.

Bishop Auckland disabled mother Annette Peareth complained in July 1995 about the length of time she and other disabled people and pensioners had to queue at Bishop Auckland post office to cash their benefits.

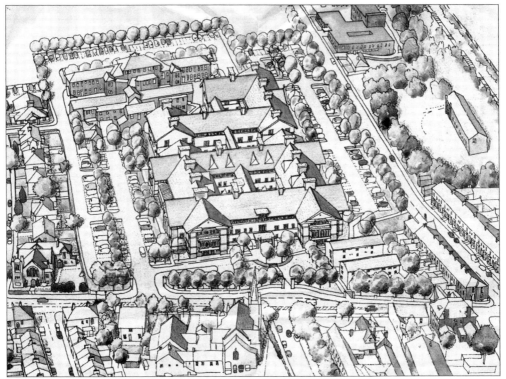

An artist's view of the redeveloped Bishop Auckland General Hospital, which is in the process of being built.

Many admittances through accidents and emergencies are brought to the hospital by ambulance personnel like Dawn Simpson, pictured here on 17 August 1988. Dawn was Bishop Auckland's first ambulance woman.

In February 1996 a new team was formed at the Hospital to run a GP out of hours care centre. Pictured here are, left to right, Fleet Manager Nigel Hopper, GP Andrew Sanderson, Patients' Manager Rowena Gill and Risk Manager Terry Holloran.

Dr Martin John gives advice over the telephone at the GP's urgent care unit at the hospital, March 1996.

These days great care is taken over hospital menus. Here hospital staff show their certificates and plaque. Left to right: Patients' Head Cook Carol Briggs, Assistant Head Cook Diane King and Staff Dining Room Head Cook Barbara Stannard ensure that the patient's inner man is well satisfied.

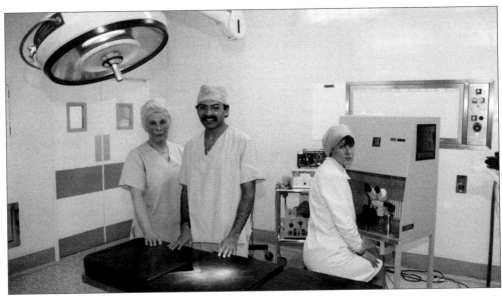

In the clinical atmosphere of the hospital's operating theatre, a patient's life is literally in the hands of the surgeon and the theatre staff. Here surgeon Mayur Chauhan is seen with theatre sister Jean Pearson, left, and Jane Bowes, the embryologist, January 1994.

When, on 27 May 1986, an appeal was launched by Bishop Auckland's General Hospital for body scanner, it got an excellent response. Many organisations devised all sorts of activities, all aimed at bringing in much needed cash. Here, left to right, Dr Shrinivas Desai, Bernard Baglee, Dr Donald Prescott and David Ryan launch the appeal.

Before the year was out the cash was rolling in. This donation by the hospital's own record department was handed over on 5 December 1986. Mrs Kathleen Hutchinson, centre, was pictured with Dr Donald Prescott (right) and secretary Bernard Baglee of the South West Durham Scanner Appeal. The hospital now has its scanner.

Dr Donald Prescott, aided by Father Christmas and friends, cuts the first sod for the scanner unit. It is Boxing Day 1987, and Father Christmas is remarkably fresh, having spent the previous night on the tiles with an old bag.

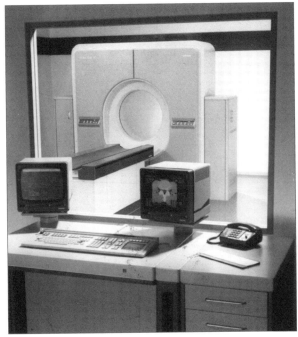

It is 9 April 1988, and there it is, the scanner unit.

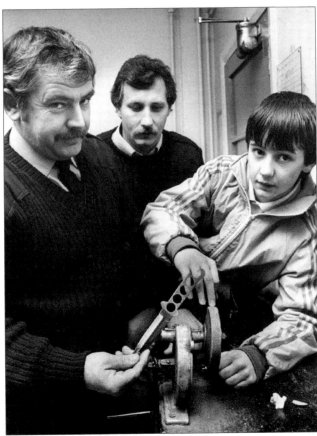

There are times when the fire service is asked to deal with what at first looks like a medical problem. When, on 19 January 1987, a Bishop Auckland boy, Steve Derger, got his finger stuck in the handle of a diver's knife, he was rescued by Sub Officer Melvyn Metcalf and Fireman Ian Armstrong of Bishop Auckland's fire service.

Lynn Brownbridge, Fire Control Operator, in relaxed mood when Bishop Auckland Fire Station held an open day, 19 August 1996.

Fighting fires is the *raison d'être* of the fire service. Here, Bishop Auckland firefighters are tackling a warehouse fire in Railway Street on 31 January 1987.

It is 1964 and Bishop Auckland Divisional Police leave their old headquarters at Bondgate to move into this new, ultra modern headquarters in the Woodhouse Close estate. The headquarters is on the left, with the Magistrates' Court block and offices on the right.

Bishop Auckland police work had to gain the trust and respect of the general public. Here, in pursuit of good relations, police horse Montrose is making friends with Christopher McKenna at a police station open day on 21 May 1985.

PC Nicky Cummings opening the door to the new foyer of Bishop Auckland police station, 28 December 1995. Criminals, in particular, are invited to enter.

A walk into the new foyer of Bishop Auckland police station could lead to time on their hands for criminals. Many law-abiding people use some of their spare time availing themselves of the manifold delights found in local libraries, such as Woodhouse Close Branch Library, seen here on 6 February 1972.

Visiting the local library is one of the many means of relaxation available to the Bishop Auckland populace, who are secure, these days, in the knowledge that a safety net provided by the DSS is always there to give people peace of mind.

Binchester, a little to the north of Bishop Auckland, was a Brigantian township and important administrative centre in pre-Roman times. When the Romans arrived they used it as a fort and important administrative centre until the fifth century AD and the site was still being used during the Middle Ages. Its importance can be judged by the magnificence of its remains, in particular its bath house which shows that the Governor of Binchester held high rank. The bath house shows the typical method of Roman bathing with connecting rooms at different temperatures. Its hypocaust, which is made of seggar brick pillars, is reputed to be one of the finest in existence. The Romans renamed Binchester *Vinovium*, and Bishop Auckland's DSS building, pictured here on 28 May 1971, is called Vinovium House.

CHAPTER SEVEN

SCHOLARSHIPS

The award-winning cross-country team of Bishop Auckland's King James I Comprehensive School, seen here on 23 December 1992, highlights this fine school's belief in the old adage 'A healthy mind in a healthy body'.

Despite its inadequacies, the nineteenth-century education system afforded ground work for those who had the ambition and determination to follow professional careers and for those who just wanted to sample the joys of reading. From 1900 scholarships for secondary education were obtainable at Bishop Auckland. But absorbing so much learning can be just too much for a little lady who only wants to paint. Clare Hunt, pictured here on 8 October 1986, is practising to become a cartoonist for the *Northern Echo*.

Playtime is a much more interesting lesson: Bishop Auckland Nursery School's first sports day, 21 June 1984.

In 1864 the only private school in Bishop Auckland opened officially, but it is likely that teaching began in this large building, which could accommodate between 200 and 300 people, some time earlier. It became known as Bishop Auckland High School, but the name was changed to Mount School in 1933. At one time the school was mixed, but when it closed in 1964 only girls, fifty of them, between the ages of four and a half and eighteen, were taught together. On reaching its century Mount School had a staff of eight teachers from primary level to GCE and advanced level subjects. When Miss M. Muir, the headmistress in 1964, could find no one to carry on, she regretfully decided that at the end of the summer term of that year the school would close. Since the school was a private one, Bishop Auckland Education Department had no responsibility for it. Parents had to make their own arrangements for the transfer of pupils to other schools.

Like doors, when one school closes another opens. Under the Education Act of 1944 the Durham County Development Plan for Secondary Education was drawn up in 1947 and approved by the Ministry of Education in 1951. Bishop Auckland was designated a centre for Catholic secondary education. Work commenced on St John's Secondary Modern School, pictured here in November 1986, in 1962. It was ready for the intake of pupils from Wolsingham, Witton Park, Willington, Crook, Tow Law, West Auckland, Shildon, Newton Aycliffe and Bishop Auckland on 7 September 1964.

Goodbye Mr Chips. Here, on 31 May 1994, Headmaster Dudley Percival makes a real song and dance out of his retirement party at Eldon Lane Junior School, encouraging his audience of young and old to join in. He took his leave after twenty-three years as headmaster at the school. 'I will miss the children', he said. 'They have all been lovely. I have had a first-rate staff. They have always been very supportive as well as the parents and the governors.' Modesty forbids adding that this is because he was an exemplary head.

WHO put the colours in the rainbow?
Who put the salt into the sea?
Who put the cold in to the snowflake?
Who made you and me?
Who put the hump upon the camel?
Who put the neck on the giraffe?
Who put the tail upon the monkey?
Who made hyenas laugh?
Who made whales and snails and quails?
Who made hogs and dogs and frogs?
Who made bats and rats and cats?
Who made ev'rything?

Who put the gold into the sunshine?
Who put the sparkle in the stars?
Who put the silver in the moonlight?
Who made the Earth and Mars?
Who put the scent into the roses?
Who taught the honey bee to dance?
Who put the tree inside the acorn?
It surely can't be chance!
Who made seas and leaves and trees?
Who made snow and winds that blow?
Who made streams and rivers flow?
God made all of these!

Dudley thought it fitting 'that I should take my leave singing my favourite hymn'. Here it is: 'Who Put The Colours In The Rainbow?'

Bishop Barrington School in the market-place was built in 1810 by Bishop Barrington (1791–1826). Financed from the uncollected revenues of the bishopric's lead mines in Weardale. it accommodated 360 boys, including 30 Bluecoat boys. The master was paid £20 per year for teaching 'thirty poor boys of the town' under Lord Crewe's Will of 1720, with £60 per annum being allotted for their clothing. This photograph of the modern school was taken on 18 February 1983.

Bishop Barrington's pupils, 1982. At the turn of the century £10,000 was spent on the school, while £5,000 was spent on buildings and sites for schools in Weardale and a similar sum on their endowment. Schools built at Frosterley, Stanhope, Eastgate, Westgate, Rookhope, St John's Chapel, Wearhead and Lanehead provided the bulk of education in Weardale for half a century. It was the first school in England to use the monitor system of teaching in which older pupils taught the younger ones.

King James I Grammar School, founded towards the end of 1604, was named after King James I of England – VI of Scotland – and has had a chequered history. It began as an endowed school and was known as a free grammar school, yet it was free to only two scholarship boys per annum. For many years its teaching remained at a very low level. As the school developed, it acquired three different groups of buildings from all ages. Sometimes boys were taught, often girls were; but today both are, for the school has been a comprehensive since 1974. Its first headmistress has only recently retired. A massive new building programme began in September 1999 to launch this 400-year-old school into the millennium. From its humble beginning, King James I Grammar School has grown into a highly successful centre of excellence. Moreover, it has recently been designated a centre of learning for physically disabled pupils. The age of enlightenment is upon us, thanks to forward looking scholastic establishments like King James I comprehensive.

In about 1900 King James I Grammar School had room for 150 boys, of whom 40 were borders. By 1902 it had only 80 pupils. To the then headmaster, Robert Bousfield, this was unsatisfactory and he did a tremendous amount to revive its reputation. By 1910 the school had 131 pupils, a fraction of those taught there today. Here, on 29 April 1994, are some of the pupils at work in the original science lab. Today 820 pupils, boys and girls, are taught in what is now called King James I Comprehensive College.

Here, on 4 December 1974, smart, intelligent pupils are leaving the new buildings of King James I Comprehensive School, striding confidently towards a worthwhile future which will soon be in their hands.

In 1982 a proposal for the merger of King James I Comprehensive and Bishop Barrington schools caused furore in Bishop Auckland. On 8 February 1982 a large protest march, which included many pupils from both schools, wound through the town. The day was won: the merger failed.

This standard of scholastic success is the aim of Bishop Auckland schools: ten As at GCSE were achieved by Fiona Caveny, pictured on 25 August 1994. Well done, Fiona!

Education does not end with school days. Here, on 2 November 1988, Lesley Teesdale, Human Relations Manager at Eaton Ltd, Newton Aycliffe, is pictured after officially opening the Open Learning Centre at Bishop Auckland Technical College. Also pictured are the College Principal Keith Byfield, centre, and Tom Young, Open Learning Co-Ordinator.

CHAPTER EIGHT

THE RAILWAY
CONNECTION

The railway lines at the entrance to Bishop Auckland, 27 July 1962. This photograph shows how important a railway centre the town had become. By the end of the 1850s there were no fewer than seven railway lines radiating from Bishop Auckland, linking it with Butterknowle, Darlington, Durham, Kirkby Stephen, Stanhope, Spennymoor and Tow Law. The last of these lines to be built was from Bishop Auckland to Durham. Building began in 1853 and the 15-mile-long line cost an amazing £300,000, most of which was spent on the construction of Newton Cap Viaduct over the River Wear.

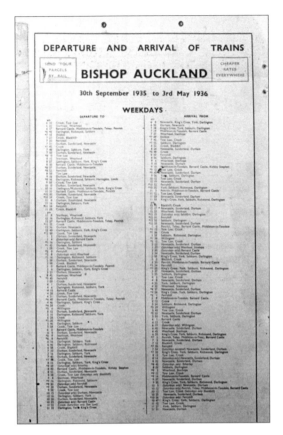

DEPARTURE AND ARRIVAL OF TRAINS

SEND YOUR PARCELS BY RAIL

CHEAPER RATES EVERYWHERE

BISHOP AUCKLAND

30th September 1935 to 3rd May 1936

WEEKDAYS

DEPARTURE TO   ARRIVAL FROM

Long before this 1936 LNER timetable was introduced the words 'coaches' and 'trains' were used outside railway parlance. A horse-drawn passenger coach, 'The Exmouth', ran between Newcastle and Lancaster. It stopped at Bishop Auckland where its passengers were put up at the Talbot Hotel, now an Iceland store. A rival coach started, and had its headquarters at the Three Tuns Inn in Newgate Street. The arrival of these two coaches was the highlight of the day with excited crowds gathering to see which coach would arrive first. Bishop Auckland's earliest trains were powered by pack horses. These pack horse trains were the main means of transporting goods, in particular lead and coal. In 1821 it was proposed to replace the pack horse trains with a tramroad from Witton Park Colliery to Stockton-on-Tees. This railway became the Stockton and Darlington Railway, which opened on 27 September 1825. A branch of the Stockton and Darlington Railway hauled coal from the Black Boy pit at Eldon.

Bishop Auckland and Darlington to Middlesbrough and Saltburn

Mondays to Fridays

					B		A								
Bishop Auckland							0742			0925	0951			1127	
Shildon							0747			0930	0956			1132	
Newton Aycliffe							0751			0934	1000			1136	
Heighington							0755			0938	1004			1140	
North Road							0805			0948	1014			1150	
Newcastle								0811	0842			1010			
Chester le Street								0821				1020			
Durham								0829	0900			1028			
Darlington a							0808	0851	0922	0952	1018	1050		1154	
Darlington d		0627	0637		0714	0753	0815	0854	0925	0954	1027	1053	1125	1156	1228
Dinsdale		0632			0719		0820						1130		
Tees-side Airport															
Allens West		0639			0726	0803	0827		0937		1037		1137		1238
Eaglescliffe		0642			0728	0806	0830		0940		1040		1140		1241
Thornaby		0647	0655		0733	0811	0835	0914	0945	1012	1045	1110	1145	1213	1246
Middlesbrough a		0653	0703		0739	0818	0841	0919	0951	1018	1051	1116	1151	1223	1252
Middlesbrough d	0635	0655		0725			0841	0921	0952	1022	1052	1116	1152	1224	1252
South Bank					0744										
British Steel Redcar					0749										
Redcar Central	0646	0706		0736	0754		0853	0933	1003	1033	1103	1128	1203	1235	1304
Redcar East	0649	0709		0739	0756		0855	0936	1006	1036	1106	1130	1206	1238	1306
Longbeck	0653	0713		0743	0800		0859	0940	1010	1040	1110	1134	1210	1242	1310
Marske	0654	0714		0744	0802		0901	0941	1011	1041	1111	1136	1211	1243	1312
Saltburn	0703	0723		0753	0810		0910	0950	1020	1050	1120	1144	1220	1252	1320

Mondays to Fridays

Fashions change, even with railway timetables. The contrast between the 1936 LNER timetable above and this 1994 one is readily apparent.

Bishop Auckland railway station, probably on a flag day, 1889. In 1881 William Crawford was the stationmaster at Bishop Auckland. He was also a composer, whose only surviving work is 'The Rokeby Polka'. He lived at the station, and his two daughters ran the station tea room. In about 1900 Bishop Auckland's 'barrow boys' gathered at the railway station with homemade carts to transport commercial travellers' samples to the various commercial hotels in the town for a fee of 1*d*. The first motorised taxis started to operate in July 1899.

A whitewashed lineside cottage with a garden at one end and a pump at the other was Bishop Auckland's first railway station. Eventually a platform was built on the site of the cottage, but it was not until 1890 that Bishop Auckland's five-platform station, shown here, was built.

In 1939 six lines spread from Bishop Auckland station; today only one, the Darlington link, remains. Pictured here on 24 October 1966, the driver of the Darlington train prepares to leave Bishop Auckland station. In 195 the line to Ferryhill through Spennymoor was closed; and in June 1953 the Wearhead service ended. In 1962 th connection with the Stainmore line to Kirkby Stephen ended, and the Barnard Castle line was closed soo afterwards. In 1964 the Durham connection was closed. Of the five services operating from Bishop Auckland i 1939, only one, from Crook to Darlington, remained in 1964. The following year the line from Bishop Aucklan to Crook closed, leaving only the 12 miles of track from Bishop Auckland to Darlington.

This diesel is standing at the only platform now in use at Bishop Auckland's once busy railway station, which was at its busiest in 1946 when 214,602 passengers used it. By 1966 this figure had dropped to 94,393 and has continued to fall, exacerbated by line closures under Beeching's axe. Insidiously the rot set in. Staff became redundant: by 1966 the six porters on each shift in 1938 had been reduced to three porters and two leading porters for both shifts. The old clocktower and the bridge to the station's platforms were dismantled in 1967. But in September 1847 the journey from Bishop Auckland to Darlington took thirty minutes; on 20 October 1966, when this picture was taken, the same journey took only twenty-three minutes, cutting the journey time by just seven minutes in 119 years!

Opposite: When the last train to 8 miles distant Crook, pictured here, left Bishop Auckland on Saturday 6 March 1965, fifty Bishop Auckland people were on board. The 125-year-old Bishop Auckland to Crook rail link was axed despite protests, petitions, meetings and enquiries, leaving hundreds of workers from Crook with a daily battle to get to work at Bishop Auckland, Newton Aycliffe and beyond. Station Foreman at Bishop Auckland, Mr Frank Rundle, who waved away the last train, said: 'This is a sad occasion. I have been here years and over the time the services to Wearhead, Barnard Castle and Tow Law have disappeared. We used to be a rail centre, but now there is just the line left to Darlington.'

It is 25 October 1984, and the diesel leaving Bishop Auckland's remaining platform is destined for Saltburn via Darlington.

A year has passed. It is 31 October 1985, and the Saltburn diesel has gone. So has the signal-box and much of the station roof window.

This view and the picture overleaf evoke the heyday of railway steam and Bishop Auckland's involvement with it. Here, in 1965, a steam train arrives from Crook and the Wear Valley line, entering a station still complete and full of life.

Passing an impressive Bishop Auckland signal gantry is A4 Pacific locomotive, No. 60004, 4–6–2 *William Whitelaw*, pulling a special train in 1965. *Mallard*, another A4 Pacific, reached a speed of 125.8 mph between Grantham and Peterborough, thus attaining a world record for steam traction that has never been broken.

CHAPTER NINE

NEWTON CAP &
THE BATTS

This print is a view of Newton Cap bank with, centre, Newton Cap bridge, which is about 500 years old. The viaduct behind is the one which carries the Bishop Auckland to Durham railway line. The viaduct is 828 ft long and has eleven arches, each with a 60 ft span. Height from the river bed to rails is 100 ft. It was built in 1856.

Skirlaw Bridge, looking downstream, 1969. It was built for Bishop Skirlaw in the late fourteenth century. In about 1900 the road was widened by putting footpaths on cantilevered girders, leaving the original parapets. The two arches are unequal, the pointed one having a 91 ft span, that of the round one being 101 ft. At one time there was a gateway at the southern end of the bridge. A stone on the western parapet is inscribed 'Edward Palfreys Leep, 1744'. Edward Palfrey was a local pugilist who fought fighting dogs and bulls as well as men. On the day of his 'leep' he was on his drunken way to fight a bull, followed by a large crowd. The fight never materialised so he began acting the fool on the battlement of the bridge and fell off. Unhurt, he climbed back on to the bridge and challenged all-comers to leap after him. Three times he leaped from the bridge, but on the third time 'dashed his brains out'. An arch of Newton Cap Viaduct is seen top right.

Newton Cap Viaduct was built to carry the Bishop Auckland branch line of the York, Newcastle and Berwick Railway over the River Wear to connect Bishop Auckland, Hunwick, Willington and Brancepeth with Durham. Work began in 1854 and the viaduct was officially opened on 1 April 1857, when it was crossed by a special train of twenty-two carriages. During its building the local soil caused problems. Because of its nature, the foundations had to be laid 20 ft below the riverbed.

This photograph, taken on 3 September 1969, shows the contrasting styles between the fourteenth-century Skirlaw Bridge and the nineteenth-century viaduct. In 1994–5 the viaduct was converted into a road bridge and this superseded Skirlaw Bridge, at feet. However, Skirlaw Bridge did not become redundant. Strong winds are frequent around the top of the viaduct and wind-measuring equipment has been installed in the centre of the viaduct, linked with the meteorological office to alert police and the county council dangerous conditions. High-sided vehicles can then be redirected, using the alternative route over Skirlaw Bridge.

Jack's Bridge, over the River Gaunless near its confluence with the River Wear on the Batts is named after a line of cottages, Jack's Row, which once stood to the south of the bridge. Most of them were swept away by the great flood of 1771 when the Wear was said to have risen 8 ft higher than at any prior or subsequent period. The bridge has an odd appearance because its eastern parapet forms part of the boundary walls of the Bishop's Deer Park.

On 20 April 1373 the Bishop of Durham granted a piece of land 80 ft long by 40 ft wide to William Shepley, a hermit, on which to build a hermitage to have for life at a rent of 1d per annum. It was sited south of Jock's Bridge, where later Jock's Row was built. Some six centuries later, in 1970, people were living on the Batts rent free. This long shot, taken from the viaduct in 1970, depicts a pleasant, peaceful scene. But all is not what it appears to be.

This is an illegal caravan site. By 1972 there were so many caravans parked on the Batts, where parking is strictly prohibited, that residents complained to Wear Valley UDC about the nuisances caused by the occupants. There were neither toilet nor washing facilities, and the fishermen complained about the fouling of the river. Wear Valley UDC took appropriate action and the caravans have gone.

A view of Newton Cap from the viaduct, 7 September 1966 – between the closure of the line on 20 June 1966 and the removal of the track.

Four years on, in 1970, the track has gone and the viaduct has been given the kiss of death. Soon it will be gone too, unless there is a change of heart.

On 19 February 1985 a meeting was held to discuss plans for the demolition of the viaduct.

There were five speakers at the public meeting held in Bishop Auckland Town Hall that fateful February evening. They discussed four alternative routes through or bypassing nearby Toronto to replace the viaduct. The speakers were, left to right, Peter Meade, John Braithwaite, Jack Flynn, Bob Pendlebury and Brian Masterman.

he viaduct was saved, and moves were made to have it converted into a motorway. As work progresses, a guided ∣our is arranged to enable the people of Bishop Auckland to see for themselves the shape of things to come. The ∣ate of the tour is 5 November 1994. Here, one member of the public has a sneak preview – there's always one – ∣efore the tour starts.

aturday 5 November 1994 was a foggy day at Bishop Auckland but there was a good turn out to see how the ∣ew motorway was shaping up. Here Stewart McPherson, representing the contractors, explains various points.

The conversion is complete and Bishop
Auckland has a spanking new and
very spectacular motorway. Before its
official opening, ramblers lined up for
the start of a charity walk which
began with a crossing of the viaduct
on 16 July 1995.

Opening day was 21 July 1995, and this vintage Austin was one of the first vehicles to cross the
newly opened Newton Cap Viaduct.

CHAPTER TEN

PUBS & CLUBS

Bishop Auckland's weekend starts after work on Friday, and these days many of the younger set spend much of it in the boisterous atmosphere of a bar or club where lager usually heads the popularity stakes. This evocative picture, taken by brilliant Northern Echo *photographer Ian Weir, at 12.45 a.m. on Saturday 21 April 1990, shows revellers pouring out of Harvey's at the end of a festive evening.*

Where converted Newton Cap Viaduct had one opening day, nearby Newton Cap public house has opened every day since before 1896, the year Cameron's bought it. Of the four public houses serving the Newton Cap Bank area in about 1900, only the Newton Cap public house, pictured here in 1993, remains. As far back as 1870 the Bishop Auckland working man's reputation as a hard drinking gambler had been long established. He believed in the sure goodness of 'beer, baccy and billiards' and felt duty bound to get roaring drunk on Saturday nights. This strong leaning towards bacchanalia prompted several temperance organisations to become established in the town, but it took many long years of scientific and philanthropic effort to make even slight inroads into checking what was, in fact, a national vice.

In those days public houses were a male province, spittoon and sawdust places which 'you went in sideways in case anyone recognised you'. Respectable women never went into public houses; but some of the 'other sort' did; and if they got pregnant they had to go to the workhouse to have their babies. How time has changed everything! Today not only do respectable ladies drink and dine alone in public houses, catering for the whole family is *de rigueur*. In these enlightened times many pubs are run by very respectable, efficient landladies like Christine Peart, who now manages the Newton Cap.

Pollard's Inn, Etherley Lane, in the latter years of the nineteenth century. It was one of more than sixty pubs in the town at the beginning of the twentieth century. At that time beer was the great palliative for almost any illness. If you felt unwell, a glass of beer would put you right: in many quarters it still does. Black beer and rum would cure a cold; and if you were off your food a gin and bitter before a meal would do the trick.

Completely rebuilt, without its original character and with encroaching dwellings closing in, Pollard's Inn has survived more than a century of change and is still going strong.

The Sun Inn had stood in High Bondgate for over 200 years along with 2 others, Court Inn and Seven Stars Inn, now gone. Early in 1981 this Newcastle Breweries pub closed, and work began on its demolition in 1982. But this was no ordinary demolition. Experts from Beamish Open Air Museum spent months photographing the derelict building to assist its accurate reconstruction at Beamish; fittings were removed and all the bricks were marked. It was a long process lasting two years, but the Sun has now risen again, as has the price of the beer.

When invited to someone's home around the turn of the century for tea or coffee, the host invariably poured a little rum or gin into the cup first: it gave the ladies a warm glow. But it was to the public houses like the King's Head in Newgate Street that men gravitated. For there 'Free and Easies' were held at which people were encouraged to sing or recite, usually in the largest room in front of packed houses. For well over a century this fine Vaux house has served Bishop Auckland well, as it still continues to do. The large canopied windows either side of the entrance have been replaced with more modern ones, but the excellent quality of the Vaux brew has remained constant. The same cannot be said of its name, which used to be the Tile Sheds Inn.

In about 1900 there was an abundance of pubs in Bishop Auckland, the heaviest concentration being in the market-place and Newton Street areas. Two of them with royal connotations stood side by side on the northside of the market-place: the Queen's Head and the King's Arms, seen here in 1985. The Queen's Head, one of Bishop Auckland's older pubs, was auctioned on 12 May 1862 by a Mr T.N. Dote to a private buyer, but it is now part of Vaux's empire. Portraits of Queens of England adorn its walls along with pictures of old Bishop Auckland. The King's Arms was renamed the Post-Chaise in 1989, but the Queen's Head remains inviolate.

A picture of Her Majesty the Queen by Dorothy Wilding over the bar at the Queen's Head, 29 January 1975.

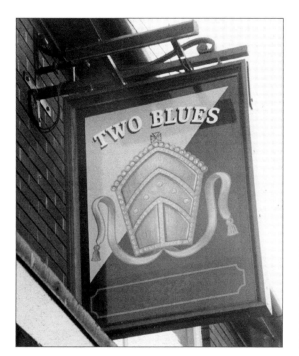

The popular Two Blues public house is only forty years old, yet it brings together the town's long association with the bishopric of Durham (symbolised by the mitre on the pub sign) and its deep involvement with football, Bishop's other religion. The Two Blues are the colours of Bishop Auckland's football team.

The Red Alligator sign commemorates Bishop Auckland's proudest racing moment, that magical day in 1968 when local jockey Brian Fletcher rode Red Alligator in the Grand National and won. At odds of 199–7 the punters had a field day – and the bookies felt a draught! Brian Fletcher had two other memorable Grand National wins, both on the same horse, which his trainer said was murder to train. That is why the horse was called Red Rum, which is murder in reverse.

The Bay Horse, Fore Bondgate, is the
oldest hostelry in County Durham. For
centuries it was owned by a member of
the Oswald-Pearson family, one of
whom, in 1579, purchased a clock.
It was still at the inn during the 1870s.
The Bay Horse is still a thriving inn,
only now it is called the Outback. It was
traditional for Bishop Auckland girls to
collect money for charity from making
mid-summer cushions. These were
made by covering stools with clay and
designing patterns on them using
flowerheads, seeds and leaves, rather
like Derbyshire well-dressing. Following
a day of fund raising, the girls held a
party in the Bay Horse.

Landlord of the Bay Horse, Tom Wright, pictured here in 1987, always had some coins lying on the
bar – not seen in this photo – but customers were unable to pick them up because they were stuck
down with strong glue. Not only does the bar have a telephone, it is inside a telephone kiosk, which
is beneath a ceiling festooned with chamber pots. All of which is confusing after a few jars.

Along with the public houses, working men's clubs thrived in Bishop Auckland. They catered for people from the same workaday environment who preferred to relax with their workmates in an unpretentious venue where they could feel at home; and drink beer at cheaper prices than those charged in the pubs. Usually, as in Cockton Hill Workman's Club, pictured here in 1979, entertainment was laid on. The chairman was somebody noted for the loudness of his voice. Should the audience become unruly, he would boom 'Order, give order, please'. It was not uncommon for a visiting artiste to be ordered to 'hurry up and finish your act. Pies and peas are nearly ready!' The chairman of a working men's club probably had many good qualities, but tact was seldom one of them.

Bishop Auckland has its share of specialist clubs, one of which, the Gun Club, has its shooting ranges in Newton Cap railway tunnel. Another is the long-established Golf Club. This photo, dated 19 November 1986, is of Major Maurice Kirby who has been a Golf Club member since 1926.

CHAPTER ELEVEN

REMEMBRANCE, DUTY & FUN

Bishop Auckland cenotaph used to stand on the approach to the town's railway station.
Here, several people are admiring the poppy wreaths laid on it on Remembrance Sunday 1939,
apprehensive, perhaps, about gathering war clouds.

Halfords and a roundabout now occupy the cenotaph's original site. It was moved to the market-place, where it now stands, in 1986. This photograph was taken shortly after the cenotaph was resited.

It is thanks to Dunkirk veterans like Ron Tivner, pictured here at the cenotaph on Remembrance Sunday 1984, that we can speak our minds with impunity and rest easy in our beds at night. He holds a wreath of Flanders poppies and wears his Second World War medals with pride. He is in reflective mood, remembering the evacuation of the BEF from the French beaches. It took place between 27 May and 3 June 1940, and according to an Admiralty communique was 'the most extensive and difficult combined operation in British naval history'.

Without a strong defence a country places its hard-won freedom in jeopardy. Here, members of Bishop Auckland's 2505 squadron of the Air Training Corps, pictured against a Liberator bomber in 1989, blend into a highly efficient team in which discipline, patriotism and service, mixed with humour, all play an important part. Through organisations like the ATC, young people are encouraged to develop into responsible citizens by serving others; they are a credit to Bishop Auckland.

Bishop Auckland General Hospital has its own radio station, pictured here on 18 February 1996, with DJ Jean White and some of the volunteers who help to run it. The station has a reassuring effect on patients and its request programmes are particularly popular.

Hospitals like Bishop Auckland General depend on the fund-raising events of many civic-minded people who willingly devote much of their spare time doing good deeds. Here, on 9 November 1982 (left to right) Gillian Greenwell, Brenda Crane, Carol Allison and Mary Waine, all members of Bishop Auckland Ladies' Circle, are fund raising for a cardiac-arrest machine for the hospital with their nearly new shop. Their target was £4,000.

These two young ladies are Bishop Auckland Technical College students fund raising for Ethiopia with a hairdressing competition, 21 December 1984.

Earlier that year the girls from St Trinian's got in on the act during Woodhouse Close Carnival,
16 July 1984.

Bishop Auckland is in a good walking area and Cauldron Snout, pictured here, is a favourite destination for walkers, who are often sponsored for local charities. It is a turbulent cataract near the source of the River Tees and one of the most striking topographical features of Upper Teesdale. Maize beck meets the River Tees at its foot.

Some people prefer al fresco fun, like the 'All-American, It's A Knockout' team from Black and Decker, 1988.

For Bishop Auckland Operatic Society it is being on the stage side of the proscenium arch that makes the adrenalin flow. Here, on 19 October 1982, the production is *Carousel*.

Pensioner Tommy Moule, a student of local history, with copies of Matthew Richley's *History and Characteristics of Bishop Auckland* (1872), 29 April 1985.

The pavilion shown here is a dual-purpose building, serving bowlers and tennis players alike.

To the east of Bishop Auckland, the River Gaunless meanders northwards through the Bishop's Park to its destiny with the Wear. All the parkland east of the Gaunless, which is most of the park, comprises High Plains Golf Course. The building shown here is the nineteenth hole, the clubhouse. Golf became established in Bishop Auckland in about 1900 and its first headquarters was the Talbot Hotel, across the road from the most prominent building in town, the drapers and outfitters, Messrs Duff and Rowntree. Three of the town's practising doctors became the Golf Club's first captains. In 1900 T.A. McCullagh was the first, in 1901 G.W. Ellis was captain (the Ellis Cup is competed for annually), and I.A. Ward was the third.

ehind this modern pavilion on the Cricket Club ground, pictured here on 20 April 1960, are more than 300 years f cricket. As early as 1660 a cricket club existed and by 1751 the game was being played in County Durham. In 773 nearby West Auckland played Scrutton for 25 guineas a side; and by the 1830s bets were placed on scratch ams from Bishop Auckland, West Auckland, and other villages and hamlets. Bishop Auckland Cricket Club was unded in 1853 'for serious cricket playing'. During the 1860s and 1870s there was much interest in cricket, hich was still very much a gentleman's game. All the games were friendlies, often attracting fairly large crowds. In 870, when the *Northern Echo* was first published, sports coverage was scanty. This began to change when, on uesday 21 June of that year, the *Northern Echo* printed a few score cards for the first time. The match was between ishop Auckland Cricket Club and Redcar & Coatham Cricket Club, and the *Northern Echo* reported that 'a match ook place between the above clubs and was played on the Bishop Auckland Ground on Saturday and resulted in an arly win for the Aucklanders by one innings and 45 runs to spare'. In October 1904 the Aucklanders applied for dmission to the North Yorkshire and South Durham League and were refused. The following year Bishop uckland was admitted to the League for the 1906 season, and this is still the one in which they still play.

emonstrating to youngsters hat playing the game is far uperior to simply being a pectator, organisations like Voodhouse Community Centre un three-day football coaching ourses. Here, Wilfred Dixon is een with the five-a-side winners, July 1985.

When it comes to fun, Bishop Auckland's children are not forgotten. Pictured outside St Anne's church on 23 July 1994, Jem Hulpert rides his unicycle as Mike Willoughby provides musical support. The twosome, called 'The Fairly Famous Family', were beginning a summer-long series of entertainments for children in Bishop Auckland.

CHAPTER TWELVE

THAT'S ENTERTAINMENT

Bishop Auckland solicitor Neville Fairclough, standing, and members of Bishop Auckland Chamber of Trade at a meeting held in July 1989 to interest the public in the foundation of a town carnival. To date Bishop Auckland still does not have the fully integrated town carnival it clearly deserves.

On 9 July 1994 there was a festival of early music at Auckland Castle. John Peel is pictured here parading in the castle grounds prior to a performance by his renaissance outfit Estampie, with his Flemish pipes.

There's nothing like ballet for adding a touch of class to a place, and Bishop Auckland's entertainment would be the poorer without it. North East Ballet and Dance Champion, Nicola Dilworth, is seen here at her new dance studio, Nicola's Hall of Dance, in Newgate Street, 27 April 1995. The pupils are Charlotte O'Connor, in the ballet dress, Katie McKenna and Lewis Heels.

allet and Flemish pipes belong to the rofessional theatre, which, in Bishop uckland, was originally centred on a large ooden hut in Fairless Street. In the 1870s andy Boyd built the Theatre Royal. In 892 Andrew Jefferson, then the lessee, ad it rebuilt at a cost of £2,000 and enamed the Eden Theatre. Jefferson ought good drama, opera and music hall Bishop Auckland and attracted excellent ouses. He had no opposition until local usinessmen built the Hippodrome Theatre Railway Street in 1909. Arthur Jefferson anaged the Eden Theatre twice: from 889 to 1896 and from 1921 to 1925. rom 1916 until he died on 7 October 917 Charles Draycott was manager of the den Theatre and his widow, Muriel, took ver its management until 1921. The Eden heatre showed films but newer cinemas ere more popular. It degenerated into ird-rate variety and finally became a ngo hall, being demolished in 1974 to ake way for a new road through town.

he sad demise of a tired old lady: the Eden Theatre's disfigured auditorium in 1974. Yet even in its death throes is once opulent theatre has a tale to tell. During its reconstruction in 1892 a workman fell from the roof and as killed. The foreman went to the man's home and said to the lady who answered the door: 'Are you Mrs X?' am Mrs X', the lady replied. 'Well now you're widow X. Your husband has just fallen off the theatre roof', the reman announced. The dear lady didn't scream, didn't become hysterical. She simply asked the foreman if he ould go next door and ask the neighbours to come in.

The Hippodrome Theatre was opened in 1909 and in 1911 Signor Pepi, the Italian impresario, took over the lease with a grand opening that included 'Captain Woodward's World Famous Performing Seals and Lions' They topped a bill containing the famous comedienne Ada Fawn and the Russel Trio and Minotti, an outstanding cycling act. Later the Hippodrome mixed live acts and silent films. The first purpose-built cinema, the King's Hall, seen here in 1964, opened in Newgate Street in December 1914, just in time to show war propaganda films.

Bishop Auckland's first films were seen in a marquee in the market-place where the audience sat on wooden benches, the projector was turned by hand and the music came from a one-legged music box. The town's first permanent cinema was The Lyric, opened in 1911. It also had live artists like Winky, Pop and Eddie, one of whom danced on his toes in outsize shoes. The Temperance Hall, now the Masonic Hall, in Victoria Street was where Pickton's Pictures were shown. Bishop Auckland had four cinemas: the Odeon, seen here in 1959, Eden Theatre, Essoldo and King's Hall.

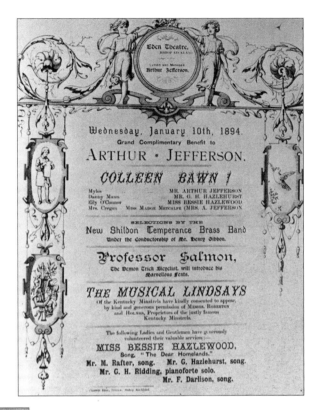

n Wednesday 10 January 1894 an Arthur
Jefferson benefit production was presented at the
Eden Theatre. In a sketch that topped the bill his
first wife, Madge Metcalfe, an accomplished actress,
played the part of Mrs Gregan. The programme,
shown here, is the oldest remaining from the Eden
Theatre. 'AJ', as his friends called him, was a
flamboyant character. He habitually stood outside
the theatre in dress suit and top hat. When the first
house came out he would wish the patrons
'goodnight', adding, 'Have you seen my lad at the
King's Hall?' His lad, of whom he was very proud,
was Stan, who later received world acclaim as the
thin one of the lovable duo Laurel and Hardy. 'AJ'
had a bad temper. He also had an office on a
corner, up a short flight of steps. On Saturday
nights the touring manager of that week's
performing company would come to the office to
collect the company's wages; and sometimes 'AJ'
would complain about the poor standard of the
show. A row would develop and 'AJ' would lose his
temper, throwing the manager down the steps. He
would then write comments in the account book for
that week. If the show was bad, he wrote 'Quoth
the raven' from Edgar Allen Poe's poem 'Quoth the
raven no more'. That company would not be
employed by him again.

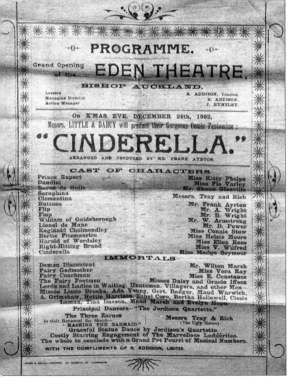

On Christmas Eve 1902 the pantomime *Cinderella*
was playing at Bishop Auckland's Eden Theatre. In
November 1926 Ivy Duke, the film-star sex symbol
who turned to straight theatre, appeared at the
Eden Theatre. During the week commencing
Monday 5 March 1945 the Canadian troubadours
Ted and Barbara Andrews, mother and stepfather of
Julie Andrews, had second billing. Variety is the
spice of life! Roy Pattinson rose from working as a
call boy at the Eden Theatre via Bishop Auckland
Operatic Society to become a professional actor and
singer. He has appeared in many West End musicals,
such as *Finnian's Rainbow, Oliver* and *Guys And
Dolls*. His TV work includes *The Likely Lads*, and
When The Boat Comes In. For more than
thirty-eight years Mrs Hetty Sutton was associated
with the theatre bar.

Stan Laurel, son of Arthur Jefferson, Bishop Auckland's much-loved son, was born in Ulverston. When he was five years old he was brought to Bishop Auckland for the christening of his sister in St Peter's church. Stan had already been christened, but, because of illness, this had taken place at his grandparent's house, so he was rechristened during the same service as his sister. When he was about six years old he became a border at King James I Grammar School, and then attended schools at Gainford and Tynemouth. In later years Stan looked back on his time in Bishop Auckland with great affection. During his early days on the stage Stan Jefferson worried about the length of his name on the billing and the fact that it contained thirteen letters. His Australian partner in his first double act, Mae Dahlberg, was looking at an etching of a Roman figure in a history book one day. The Roman was wearing bay leaves and Mae mistook them for laurel. She suggested that their act be called Stan and Mae Laurel. Stan mouthed the word several times, then nodded agreement. 'Sounds good', he pronounced and Stan Laurel was born.

Here Laurel and Hardy are seen at the height of their fame in 1942. In 1960 Stan was given a special Academy Award 'for his creative power in the field of cinema comedy'. He died in 1965 having never given up his British citizenship. On 30 April 1988 a pilgrimage of 150 'sons' from 15 British fan club 'Tents' gathered in Bishop Auckland for the tenth National Convention of The Sons Of The Desert. It was organised by John Land. Along with affiliated groups from Europe, these enthusiastic members of the legendary duo's fan club paraded through Bishop Auckland, passing the site of the old Eden Theatre, which Stan's father managed, and calling at King James I Comprehensive, which was a grammar school in Stan's day. They carried banners, wore fezzes and red sashes, had a band and a lunch and a good time was had by all. The Bishop Auckland 'Tent' is called 'The Hog Wild Tent' and its Grand Vizier is a very beautiful lady, Gillian Wales.

This MGM poster advertises the Laurel and Hardy film *Double Whoopee*, their twenty-ninth film. Arthur Jefferson wanted his son to have a front-of-house career, but Stan insisted on being a performer. He developed his talent by visiting north-east music halls and observing people, and made his theatrical debut in Glasgow when he was sixteen. He established himself touring America with Fred Karno's outfit in 1913. His partnership with Oliver 'Babe' Hardy, who was famed for his genteel pomposity, began in 1926 when he became the thin half and gag advisor of the Laurel and Hardy team.

Before league football, Bishop Auckland Church Institute, Darlington and Sunderland were the major teams in Durham; and in Bishop Auckland's case it all began when youths kicking a 'ball' of rags in the market-place broke the vicarage window. As a consequence of this, Bishop Lightfoot persuaded graduates who had come to the Bishop's Palace to be 'finished off' before taking up positions as clergy in the diocese to start a football club. The clubs colours, 'the two blues', were chosen by the Revd Mr Eden, Vicar of Bishop Auckland, because the students all came from either Oxford or Cambridge. The club was formed in 1882. In the 1885–6 season they won the Durham Challenge Cup, beating Birtley 3–1 at Feethams, Darlington. The players, shown here but not in order, were H. Waters, R. Theakstone, R. Stachan, J. Dowling, A. Foster, J. Buchanan, E. Fairless, J. Bryson, E.F. Every, J.G. Stachan and G.W. Pallister. In 1887 the club took a hard blow from which it never really recovered. The Durham Challenge Cup Committee said that some players had behaved in a manner calculated to bring disgrace to the name of the Durham Football Association and six players were suspended from taking part forever in any fixtures with any affiliated Durham FA club. This led to the Bishop Auckland Cricket Club starting a soccer team, Bishop Auckland Town. By the end of the 1886–7 season the new club was playing on the Flatts Farm ground. This new club was later to become world famous as Bishop Auckland Football Club. On 26 March 1887, when Auckland Town played its first ever game against Newcastle East End, later to become Newcastle United, no fewer than eight former Institute players were included in the side, which lost 2–7. The Institute needed nine replacements and at the height of the crisis the church club was unable to field a team for the semi-finals of the County Cup, giving Darlington a walkover.

Pride is written on the faces of the Bishop Auckland AFC players pictured here at the end of the 1938–9 season. They were winners of the FA Amateur Cup, Northern League Championship and Durham Challenge Cup. The game of soccer in 1938 had changed considerably since the 1880s. In those early days there were neither nets nor cross bars, just a tape or a clothes line. There was no centre circle, no halfway line, no free kicks or penalties. The teams changed ends after every goal and players did not have numbers on their jerseys: they were identified by their different coloured or quartered caps. They wore trousers, referred to as knickerbockers or knickers, which later became pants or shorts. Footwear was more akin to pit boots. The team's formation was goalkeeper, full back, half back, and eight forwards. Soccer was a dribbling game: when a player got the ball he ran with it towards his opponent's goal until either he scored or was dispossessed, usually by 'hacking', kicking at his shins. This practice was eventually outlawed.

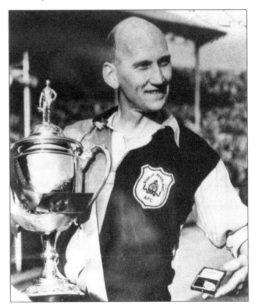

Bishop Auckland AFC has produced many famous footballers, including its most famous son, Bob Hardisty, pictured here at Wembley on 16 April 1955. He captained the team to the amateur cup victories of 1956 and 1957, and is commemorated by a road bearing his name.

Lord Tedder, Marshal of the RAF, shakes hands with the Bishop Auckland team before the start of the Amateur Cup final at Wembley, April 1956. Following the game the winning team, 'the Two Blues', was presented to Lord Tedder. Up to 1985 the team has been in the first round proper nineteen times, the second round nine times and the fourth round once.

'The Bishops' versus Hendon at Wembley, 1955. The nickname 'The Bishops' is a reminder that three former Bishop Auckland players went on to become bishops of the church: E.F. Every, Bishop of the Falkland Islands; G.R. Eden, Bishop of Wakeland; J.R. Harmer, Bishop of Dorchester. Bishop Auckland football team won the FA Amateur Cup ten times, a record.